CW01655743

Passionate about Plants

By Betty Mills

for
Sandra
from
Betty Mills

Published by Coast and Country Productions Ltd

Passionate about Plants

Passionate About Plants was first published in Great Britain in April 2009 by Coast and Country Publications Ltd, Tyldesley House, Clarence Road, Llandudno, Conwy LL30 1TW. Tel 01492-870883. www.coastandcountrymagazine.co.uk

Published, promoted & distributed by Coast and Country Productions Ltd in association with Ads2life: www.ads2life.co.uk

This paperback edition was first published in April 2009.

A catalogue record for this book is available from the British Library.

Paperback edition ISBN 978-1-907163-00-5

Edited by Don Hale OBE. Typeset and designed by Katie Gatton BA.

Printed and bound by Cambrian Printers, Llanbadarn Road, Aberystwyth, SY23 3TN.

Passionate about Plants

Yes, I suppose I am! Nowadays I am described as a Designer, Wild Flower Artist, Needlewoman and Diarist. This covers a wide range of artistic activity and I have enjoyed it all throughout a long and varied career. In recent years I have turned to serious wild flower drawing which led to an interest in Nature Conservation which has encourged the keeping of illustrated Diaries.

It has all certainly made the time go quickly and I am delighted now to have the opportunity to compile this book and share some of my interests with as many people as possible.

The work herein is drawn from three slender Collectors' books produced at Pensychnant Nature Conservation Centre in North Wales, where both the Celebration of Weeds and the Alphabet of Wildflowers, amongst other pictures of mine, formed the centres of two exhibitions.

"The Five Diaries" original book was prepared as a compilation of work done in Diary form from 1989 to 2003. It is included here almost in its entirety, its original introduction being self-explanatory.

The same applies to "the Alphabet of Wildflowers".

However, "The Celebration of Weeds" has been specially edited for this book with a new introduction and comments.

A simple, comprehensive Index, covering all three books, is included with various extra notes.

I hope you enjoy it all, and feel encouraged to go out and seek the beauty of wild plants in the area where you live.

Betty Mills
February 2009

Contents

Page

An Iris Foetidissima flower with, behind l to r: Woodsage & Foxglove and foreground Creeping Cinquefoil

Five Diaries

Introduction

This is a book about beauty, not botany and expresses a designer's fascination with the shape and colour of all plants. It is intended to encourage those with an interest in the natural world to take a closer look at plants: trees, shrubs and climbers; annual, bi-ennial and perennial flowering plants; ferns, fungi, moss and lichen. In fact, everything that grows in soil or on things that grow in soil both wild, indigenous and, sometimes, cultivated.

The five diaries of the title are all records of time spent looking at and recording in paint, pencil, ink and crayon - as well as with a camera - plants in quite small areas around and adjacent to the Conwy Estuary in North Wales.

A few of the plants are unique to the area. Many are only found in seaside areas or on limestone. Some plants quite common in other parts of the U.K. are not found here at all and not all that grows here is recorded (certainly not the sea-shore plants which are barely touched upon).

The illustrations in this book have been specially prepared and are drawn from - in both senses of the word - the five diaries which are:

The Flowers on a Path
August 1989 - July 1990

A record of 105 varieties of plants growing alongside a footpath through an S.S.S.I. at Deganwy on the shores of the Estuary opposite Conwy town. This site is part of the Vardre, an outcrop of rocky hills once crowned by a Castle. Outstanding plant: MAIDEN PINK.
A bound book of cartridge paper, A4 in size, 92 pages.
Mostly pencil and crayon with some tinted paper added and six photographs by M.J. Mills.
A Full Index with Latin names and a list of Plant Families.
Code used throughout this book to indicate plants recorded in this diary: FP
Right: the footpath looking towards Conwy.

Pensychnant Diary 1996

A record of a year's regular visits to the Pensychnant Nature Conservation Centre at the top of the Sychnant Pass behind Conwy town. About 200 plants recorded with special notes on Ferns, Fungi, Moss, Lichen and Grass. Outstanding: TREE BLOSSOM.
Another bound book of Cartridge paper, A4 in size, 124 pages, no photos.
Mainly pencil and crayon drawings plus a detailed map, drawing of the house and Full Index.
CODE in this book: PS. See page 6 for picture and Map on page 7.

A Churchyard Diary
1999

Plants and Flowers found every Sunday - plus a note about the weather - in St. Hilary's Churchyard, Llanrhos (a couple of miles inland from Deganwy on the way to Llandudno.
More than 150 plants recorded with a number of special notes on varieties, especially grasses.
Outstanding impressive displays of Snowdrops, Primroses & Bluebells.
A "pocketed" loose-leaf book using cartridge, water colour and tinted papers back to back in pockets. A4 in size, 72 pages (36 pockets). Pencil and crayon, ink and water colour. Many photographs by M.J. Mills within the text. Detailed map and Full Index. Laser colour copies were made.
CODE: CY

Above: St Hilary's in winter.

Diary of an Eightieth Year 2001

A self-indulgent personal record of plants seen and enjoyed thoughout the year in the whole of the area concerned.
Over 150 plants - many of them cultivated - are recorded.
A stiff-covered, ring-back book of Cartridge paper, A3 in size, 100 pages. Pen & pencil drawings with crayon. Many photos by M.J. Mills, some purely scenic. Simple Index.
CODE: 80

The Flowers on a Path II May 2002 - April 2003

A twelve-month record of the flowers and plants alongside the Invalid's Walk on the lower south side of the Great Orme at Llandudno. The Walk extends to the West Shore from the well-tended Haulfre Gardens. This is a Limestone area and both the Common and Hoary Rockrose grow in profusion.
A stiff-covered ring-back book of cartridge paper 11" square, 100 pages. Pen, pencil & crayon. Photos by M.J. Mills.
About 130 plants recorded.
Simple Index.
CODE: IW

Right: The Invalid's Walk looking towards the West Shore.

These photographs and those on the two previous pages are by Maurice J. Mills who is, of course, Betty Mills's husband; his work is an integral part of four of the Five Diaries, where it is particularly effective in the Diary of a Churchyard.

Above:
The Conwy Estuary on a Summer's day. Taken from the Great Orme above the Invalid's Walk.

Left:
Pensychnant Nature Conservation Centre on a Winter's Day. The house is on the left against the trees of the Home Wood. The Estate, which includes a 30 acre working farm, extends to a total of 150 acres of mountain & woodland.

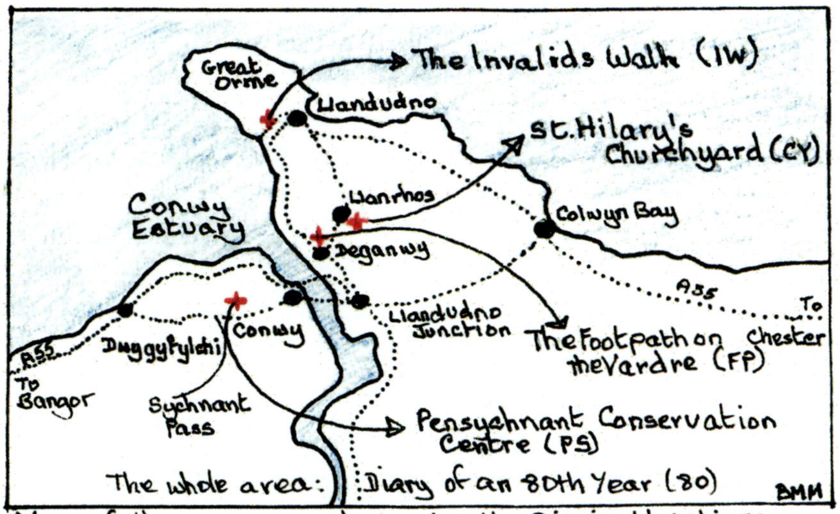

Map of the area covered showing the Diaries' locations.

GRASSES: gramineae and RUSHES: juncaceae

Both groups of plants are difficult to identify precisely being specialised fields - as are Ferns, Fungi, Mosses and Lichen (all included in this book). There are more than 150 species of wild grass in the U.K. plus all cereals and grass grown for hay, silage and grazing. All five diaries feature various grasses, but only the Pensychnant Diary includes some of the 30 odd U.K. species of Rush.

SPECIES OF GRASS RECORDED:
Cocksfoot, Crested Dogstail, Bent Grass, Fescues, Meadow Grass, Hair Grass, Purple Moor Grass, Quaking Grass, Timothy, Wild Barley, Yorkshire Fog, and half a dozen more, unidentified.

January

Starting a restricted area plant diary in January is both fascinating and challenging. There are no leaves on the deciduous trees, the shapes of the evergreens are clear and dominant, the grass and the bracken (if there is any) has died back and the flowering plants are dormant. The shape of the ground shows up: paths are obvious, rocks and scree are unobscured and the views looking outward are unrestricted. Details begin to show up: moss at its greenest; tree bark patterns and colours; old flower seedheads; curly, dead leaves underfoot.

With each visit to the area concerned new growth is spotted: new shoots of bi-ennial Alexanders. Wild Arum leaves about three inches tall; tiny leaf buds on a Burnet Rose; black buds on an Ash tree and the odd, very early, Spring flower. Bushes and early flowering trees begin to show colour, mainly in the Parks and Gardens. Particularly in the Churchyard and in the lightly manicured garden round the house at Pensychnant.

Illustrated opposite:
Yew and Prunus (CY), Jasmine and Mahonia (PS), Beech buds (PS) and Alder "cones" and catkins (PS & 80)

Recorded in the Diaries for January:

TREES: Mostly buds.
Alder, Beech,
Blackthorn,
Chestnut,
Larch,
Oak (Turkey),
Pine (Cones),
Prunus (flowers),
Sycamore,
White Poplar,
Yew.

LICHEN, FUNGUS, BARK and Moss (PS)

BUSHES & CLIMBERS:
Bramble
Cotoneaster (berries & blossom)
Garrya Elliptica
Ivy (leaves & berries)
Jasmine
Mahonia
Rhododendron
Skimmia (berries)
Viburnum (flowers)

FLOWERS: Mostly leaves except F for flower.
C Alyssum F
Alexanders
Arum
Bittercress, Hairy
Buttercup
Celandine, lesser F
Daisy F
Goosegrass
Gorse F
Herb Robert
C Heathers, various F
Iris Foetidissima, Fruit
Ling F
Nettle,
Plantain
Primrose F
Red Clover
Snowdrop F
(Cultivated: C)

Total number of plants recorded in each diary for January:
FP 5, PS 19, CY 11, 80 11, IW 7.

Herb Robert & Daisy

Betty Mills

February

Snowdrops: GALANTHUS NIVALIS (family: Daffodil: AMARYLLIDACEAE) often called "The Fair Maid of February", are, of course, the flowers of the month. They grow well in the Conwy area, propagating themselves to carpet the woods. The locations in which they appear in three of the diaries (PS, CY and 80) are well wooded areas, particularly in St Hilary's Churchyard where they present a superb display.

Mosses and Lichen.

Both non-flowering plants and both propagated by types of spore or capsules.

There are 14,000 species of Moss in the world, 600 of them in the U.K.

Of Lichen there are 1355 U.K. species with 500 of them growing on shrubs and trees.

So these are very specialised fields only touched on in the Five Diaries. The winter months are the best times to see them when there is less other vegetation.

Illustrated opposite - with Snowdrops in the centre of the drawing: Top left: LICHEN of the genus USNEA on a ~~Blackthorn~~ twig and a small piece of a similar type of Lichen on a small tuft of Moss. Bottom right, a beautifully coloured, very decorative piece of LICHEN of an unidentified genus.

Top right are two mosses: THUIDIUM TAMARISCINUM with, below it, a spiky Moss of the POLYTRICHUM type.

Bottom left: a remarkably feathery and fern-like moss, probably FISSIDENS TAXIFOLIUS. All mosses and lichen illustrated from Pensychnant Woods. In the other diaries there are two kinds of Moss on tombs in the Churchyard, several more at Pensychnant and various kinds beside the Invalid's Walk.

ALSO RECORDED IN THE DIARIES THIS MONTH:

TREES: Alder, Ash, Birch, Elder, various Evergreens (conifer + cupressus). Larch, Lime, Oak & Service Tree.

BUSHES & CLIMBERS: Berberis, Burnet Rose, Honeysuckle, Ivy berries, Japonica flowers.

FLOWERS - in flower: Alexanders, Crocus, Coltsfoot: at its best, Dandelion, Daffodils, Lesser Celandine and Bittercress leaves.

GRASSES & RUSHES: some old seedheads and some new growth.

Total number of plants in each diary this month: FP 3, PS 12, CY 4 (+trees) 80 6, IW 7.

Dandelion: TARAXACUM VULGARE

Coltsfoot: TUSSILAGO FARFARA

Betty Mills

March

Things really begin to happen in March. As the days move towards the first day of Spring on the 21st., and British Summer Time begins, the heart lifts at the reassuring sign of the seasons in their appointed order.

Illustrated, right, are some of the most familiar harbingers of Spring:

Daffodils – in the wild: NARCISSUS PSEUDONARCISSUS (One of the Emblems of Wales. In the wild they are smaller, daintier and, usually, all one colour); Sweet Violets: VIOLA ODORATA; White Violets: VIOLA ALBA; Lesser Celandines: RANUNCULUS FICARIA and Primroses: PRIMULA VULGARIS. At the Top: Blackthorn: PRUNUS SPINOSA, in full flower before the leaves are open.

Recorded in the Diaries for March: in addition to the above:

TREES:
Alder, Catkins;
Almond, flowers;
Elder, buds;
Hawthorn, buds;
Holly, flower buds;
Larch; Poplar;
Sycamore,
Willow.

MOSSES etc.
Various

BUSHES:
Flowers –
Flowering Currant;
Forsythia;
Rosemary.
Buds & leaves –
Clematis;
Laurel; Skimmia;
Tea Tree.
Ivy berries.

FLOWERS:
Arum leaves; Alexanders, flowers;
Bittercress & Celandine, Lesser – flowers;
Cranesbills; Daisy; Hawkweed;
Heather; Herb Robert, flowers;
Iris Reticulata, flower;
Muscari, flowers;
Nettle leaves; Red Dead Nettle;
Speedwells & Spring Squill – flowers,
Rock Rose – early flowers;
Wall Rocket – flowers;
Woodsage leaves.

Total number of plants in each Diary This month:
FP: 10, PS: 9, CY: 7, BO: 13, IW: 12.

A Bud and new leaves of Sycamore and Ivy berries   BMM

Betty Mills

April

This is the month when variations in flowering times become apparent. For example, Bluebells are well and truly out in the Churchyard, but it is May before they appear at Pensychnant with their accompanying Stitchwort and Red Campion. But there is so much to illustrate in the next few months so a little "artist's licence" has been used and here they all are!

Illustrated, right:

Bluebell: ENDYMION NONSCRIPTUS with Wood Anemone: A. NEMOROSA, Red Campion: SILENE DIOICA and Greater Stitchwort: STELLARIA HOLOSTEA.

Also outstanding this month are the Wild Arum flowers and the increasing Blossom on trees, notably the Wild Cherries.

ALSO RECORDED IN THE DIARIES FOR APRIL:

TREES:
Ash
Blackthorn
Chestnut
Hawthorn
Larch
Magnolia stellata
Oak
Poplar
Prunus
Rowan
Sycamore
Whitebeam
Willow
Hornbeam
Privet

BUSHES:
Bilberry
Bramble
Currant Flwg.
Dewberry
Dog Rose
Honeysuckle
Ivy
Japonica
Laurel
Rhododenron

FERNS & BRACKEN at PS.

FLOWERS:
Alexanders
Aubretia
Alyssum
Barren strawberry
Bindweed, Hedge
Bittercress
B'foot Trefoil
Buttercup
Chickweed
Celandine, Lesser
Comfrey
Carline Thistle
Crpg. Cinquefoil
Daffodil
Daisy
Dogs Mercury
Dandelion
Forget-me-Not
Fumitory
Figwort
Arum
Fritillaria
Garlic Mustard
Goosegrass
Groundsel
Hawkweed
Hawksbeard
Hogweed
Horsetail
Ivy-leaved Toadflax
Muscari
Mustard
Plantain
Rock Roses
Ramsons
Sowthistle
Speedwells
Violet, sweet
Vetch, common
Wallflower
Wood Sorrel
Wood Anemone
Woodsage
Yellow Archangel
Horseshoe & Kidney Vetch
Eyebright

Total number of plants in each diary for this month:
FP 19, PS 32, CY 16, BD 15, IW

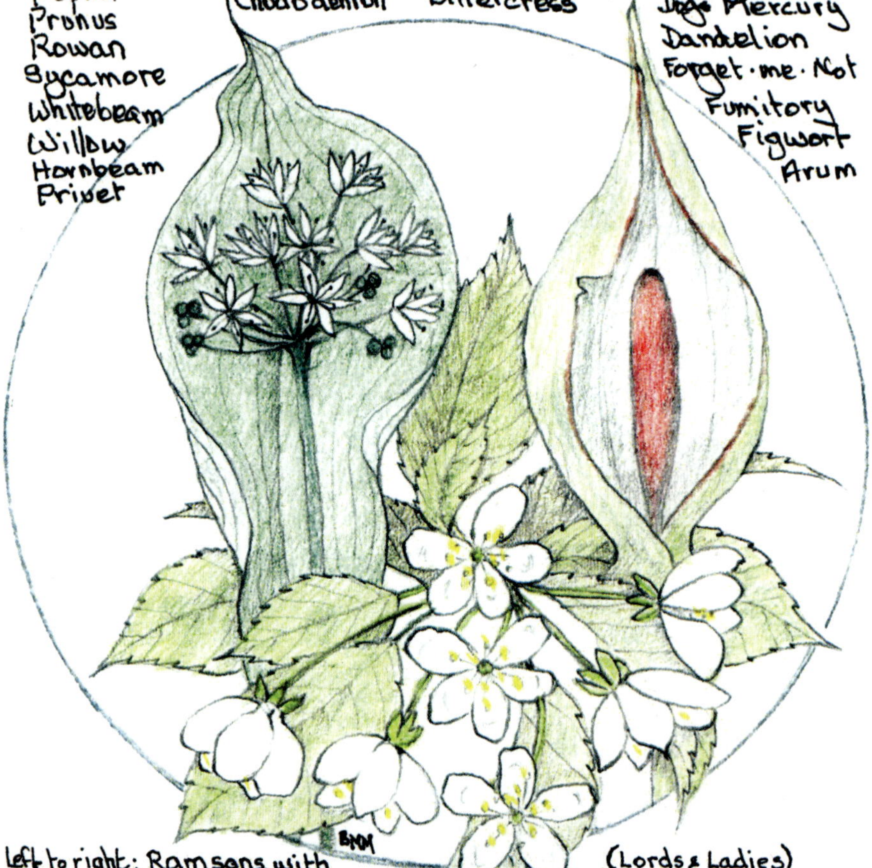

Left to right: Ramsons, with Wild Cherry or Gean (Lords & Ladies) and Wild Arum

Betty Mills

May

In May and during the following three months new flowers appear in rapid succession and keeping up with them requires some dedication. Many reappear in the same diary for several months and the different flowering times in the various locations mean that the spread of recording over the five diaries is quite wide. This shows very clearly how growing position – in this case from one side of the Estuary to the other, whether facing North or South, on a hillside or under trees – affects flowering times.

Illustrated right: Twelve flowers for May:

Top row, left to right:
Hawthorn, Lady's Smock (or Cuckoo Flower) and Crab Apple.

2nd row. l to r:
Ox-eye Daisy, Kidney Vetch and Common Fumitory.

3rd. row. l to r:
Eyebright, Burnet Rose and Maiden Pink.

Bot. row:
Spring Squill, Cambrian Poppy and Four types of Speedwell: Germander, Field, Thyme-leaved and Lilac Ivy-leaved.

Also recorded in the Diaries for May:

TREES:
Beech, Camellia,
Chestnut flower,
Elder
Field Maple flower,
Hazel, Holly flower buds,
Laburnum & Laurel flowers
Lime, Maple.
Magnolia Soulangeana flwr.
Oak flowers, Pine,
Pear flowers, Spruce,
Sycamore flowers,
Willow, Whitebeam flowers.

BUSHES: Berberis (various), Cotoneaster, Dewberry, Tea Tree, Travellers Joy.

FLOWERS:
Alexanders; Alkanet,
Bluebell; Bindweed,
Buttercup,
Birdsfoot Trefoil
Black Medick,
Clovers, Red & white.
Campion, Sea
Columbine; Cranesbills,
Cow Parsley,
Creeping Cinquefoil,
Corydalis; Cowslip,
Corn Salad; Daisy,
Foxglove; Forget-me-Not,
Ground Ivy; Horsetail,
Herb Robert,
Hedge Mustard,
Honesty,
Helianthemum (Cultv)
Herb Bennet; Lamium (c)
Medicks, various
Marsh Marigold,
Plantain; Ramsons,
Red Valerian,
Rocket, Wall,
Shepherds Purse,
Sorrel, Pink
Rosie Roses: Hairy + Common
Stitchwort,
Salad Burnet,
Thale Cress + Thyme.
Vetch, Common
Violet: Dog + Sweet
Woodruff; Watercress,
Wallflower.

Total number of plants in each diary for May:
FP 12, PS 7, CY 15,
80 19, IW 20
73 in all.

Sycamore Flower
Three Cranesbills: l to r. Small Flowered, Hedgerow & Dovesfoot
BMM

Betty Mills

June

The most outstanding flower in June is GOATSBEARD or Jack-go-to-bed-at-noon, which it actually does. Illustrated opposite, the symmetrical beauty of the seed-head, closing and opening flower and long leaves is clearly shown.
Also pictured from top right: Honeysuckle, Meadow Vetchling and Dog Rose with Lady's Bedstraw, Bird's-foot Trefoil and Restharrow from the lower left.
Four other fascinatingly-shaped flowers this month are: Ragged Robin, Bristly-Ox-tongue, Ivy-leaved Toadflax and Woodsage.

RECORDED IN THE DIARIES FOR JUNE:

TREES:
Beech, Hawthorn, Hemlock, Portugese Laurel and Privet;
Flowers on: Holly, Lime, Rowan and Whitebeam;
Early fruit on: Blackthorn, Elder, Oak and Sycamore.

BUSHES:
Ceanothus, Montana Rubens and Rhododendron;

GRASSES ETC.:
Bracken, Moorgrass, Wild Barley and Yorkshire Fog.

FLOWERS:
Bell Heather, Bindweed (various), Black Medick, Buttercup ("), Bush Vetch, B-leaved Willowherb, Corn Mint, Caraway, Catsear, Cranesbill (various), Carline Thistle, Clover (Red + White), Campanula, Creeping Cinquefoil, Crpg. Thistle, Common Rockrose, Dropwort, Daisy, Dock (various) Eyebright, Foxglove, Goosegrass, Gtr. B'foot Trefoil, Harebell, Hop Trefoil, Hogweed, Heath Bedstraw, Herb Bennet, Hawkweed, Herb Robert, Hairy Tare, Hedge Woundwort, Iris Foetidissima, Knapweed, Knotgrass, Mouse-ear, Mallow, Milkwort. Nettle, Nipplewort, Pellitory of the Wall, Red Valerian, Smith's Cress, Speedwells, Stonecrop, Sheeps Sorrel, Tormentil, Thyme and Weld.

. Total number of plants in each diary:
FP: 28; PS: 28; CY: 24; 80: 24; IW: 12.

Betty Mills

July

New flowers this month - the one with the largest number of recorded flowers over all five diaries - include those illustrated right:
Thistles are at their best in July: top left is Slender Thistle and, bottom right, the majestic Spear Thistle.
Tree blossoms are represented by the Broad Leaved Lime flowers, top right and Bushes by Bramble flower, bottom left.
Top centre: glorious Blue Lettuce from the West Shore Dunes and, bottom centre, Three Willowherbs: l to r. Broad Leaved, Great Hairy and Rosebay.
Centre left: Field Scabious from the Great Orme and, right, the ubiquitous Red and White Clover.

ALSO RECORDED IN THE DIARIES FOR JULY:

TREES:
Ash fruit,
Beech mast,
Chestnuts,
Elder flwrs + fruit,
Holly green berries,
Laburnum seeds
Oak acorns,
Privet flowers,
Silver Poplar,
Sycamore.

BUSHES:
Bilberries,
Honeysuckle flwrs,
Ivy

FERNS:
Bracken; Rustyback.

GRASS:
Yorkshire Fog.

FLOWERS:
Chickweed
Carline Thistle
Catsear
Cranesbills
Crpg. Cinquefoil
Dropwort
Dock
Foxglove
Goosegrass
Hop Trefoil
Hogweed
Harebell
Heather, Bell
Ivy leaved Bell Flower
Ivy Broomrape
Knapweed, Lesser
Ladies Bedstraw
Lucerne
Melilot, Ribbed
Mallow
Mayweed, Sea + Pineapple
Marjoram
Meadowsweet
Nettle
Nipplewort
Navelwort
Ox-tongue, bristly
Red Valerian
Rest harrow
Rose, Dog
St John's Wort
Sow thistles
Stonecrop, English
Silverweed
Self-heal
Stitchwort
Spearwort, Lesser
Tormentil
Tutsan
Thistle, Creeping
Vetchling, Meadow
Lettuce, Wall
Wood sage
Yarrow

TOTAL number of plants recorded in the diaries for July:
FP 19, PS 45, CY 13,
80 19, IW 22 118 in all

foreground: Wild Thyme. l to r: Catsear, Common Rockrose, Milkwort & Carline Thistle.

Betty Mills

August

A change comes over the diaries in August. Certain flowers are at their best: Yarrow, Ragwort, Harebells Travellers Joy, Fennel, Hedge Bindweed and Toadflax. Ferns are at their most opulent, Dandelions continue to flower, Pellitory-of-the-Wall riots more than ever and Gorse is still golden. If the Broad-Leaved Helleborine (a member of the Orchid family) is going to make an appearance at Pensychnant this is when it does.
But some trees and grasses are looking a little tired after the excesses of July and fruit and seedheads are beginning to appear. The first of these is usally Rowan berries with unripe Sloes on the Black Thorn and green seeds on Sycamore.
Illustrated right are:
Three Bindweeds: Small, Sea and, the largest, Hedge; with Blue Harebells, Blue/Pink Vipers Bugloss, White Yarrow and Yellow Ragwort.

OTHER PLANTS RECORDED IN THE DIARIES FOR AUGUST:

TREES:
Cones, Various
Elder
Eucryphia
Hawthorn
Oak
Silver Poplar
Whitebeam
Yew

BUSHES:
Bramble fruit
Dewberry fruit
Gorse
Tree Heather
Spiraea

FERNS & FUNGI etc.
Puff Balls
Champignons
Field Mushrooms

FLOWERS:
Some Rushes + Wild Barley
AND
Arum; Asters;
Alexanders;
Burnet Rose;
B'foot Trefoil;
Burnet Saxifrage;
Catsear;
Clovers
Campanula
Crpg. Cinquefoil
Dock, curled
Estherides
Fuschia
Hawkweed
Hogweed
Hypericum
Horehound, Black
Heathers
Knotgrass
Knapweed
L. Bedstraw
Mousear
Mugwort
Nettle, stinging
Nettle, Hemp
Iris Foetidissima
Parsley, Hedge
Rockrose
Thistle, Spear
Thistle Crpg.
Tormentil
+ Trailing
Willowherb, R.bay
Woodsage
Wild Thyme
Wild Carrot
Wormwood, Sea
and a Robin's Pincushion on a Dog Rose bush.

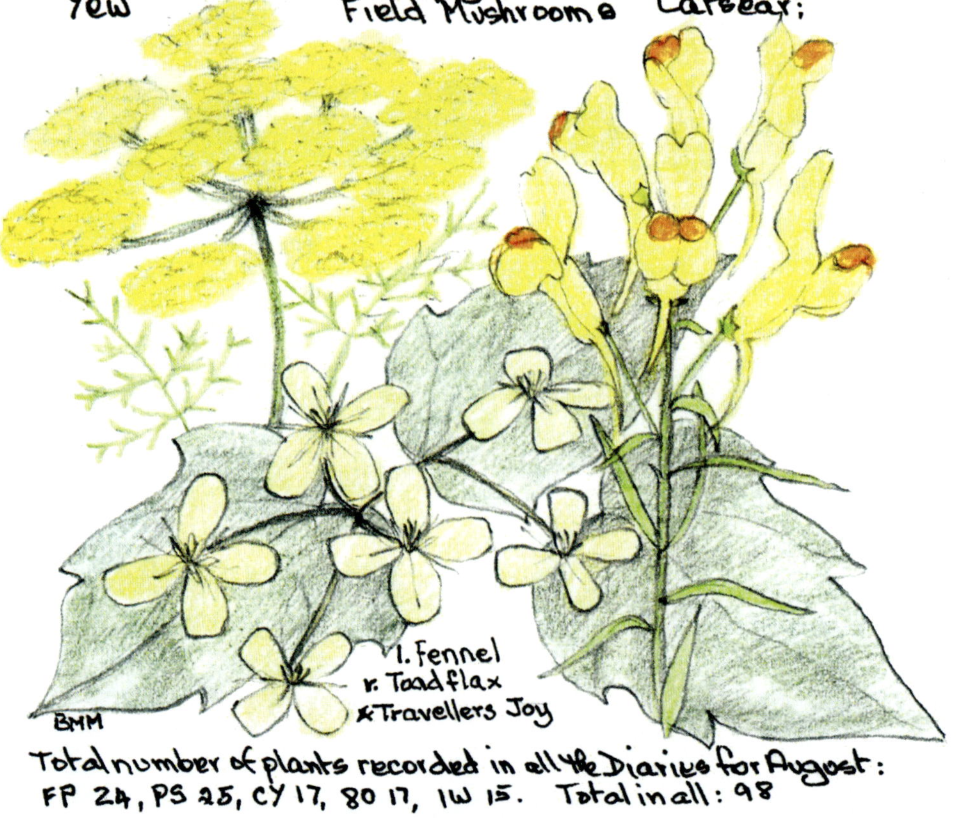

l. Fennel
r. Toadflax
& Travellers Joy

BMM

Total number of plants recorded in all the Diaries for August:
FP 24, PS 25, CY 17, BO 17, IW 15. Total in all: 98

Betty Mills

September

"Season of mists and mellow fruitfulness." To Autumn by John Keats 1819

Not always misty in this area but certainly full of mellow fruitfulness!

It was difficult to choose which fruit to illustrate, right, but, in the end, nine trees and bushes were irresistible:

Clockwise from top right: Haws, Lime fruits, Blackberries, Crab Apples, Cotoneaster berries from the Great Orme, Chestnuts from Pensychnant, Rose Hips, Sea Buckthorn berries from the West Shore and, top left, Elderberries.

Flowers are mostly represented by seedheads such as Thistledown but Common Catsear is still flowering boldly. Other plants are producing second and, sometimes, third lots of flowering.

Climbers produce quite dramatic seedheads like the long trailing stems of red-berried White Bryony and fluffy Travellers Joy.

ALSO RECORDED IN THE DIARIES FOR SEPTEMBER:

TREES:
Beech, mast
Black cherries
Cones, various
Norway Maple
Snowberries
Rowan fruit
Service Tree fruit
Strawberry tree: ARBUTUS - fruit

FERNS in the Churchyard
LICHEN & FUNGUS at Pensychnant

FLOWERS:
Alexanders: seedheads,
Agrimony: late flower,
Bluebell: seedhead,
Bindweed, Hedge: still flowering,
Clover flowers,
Dock, brd.leaved: seeds,
Hedge Mustard: seeds,
Harebell: late flower,
Herb Robert: seeds,
Hogweed: seeds,
Honesty: seeds,
Meadowsweet: seeds,
Montbretia: flowers,
Marjoram: flower,
Ragwort: seedhead,
Rock Rose, common: still flowering;
Storksbill: late flower;
Spearmint: flower;
Scabious, late flower;
Thistledown: Spear and Creeping Thistles;
Thistle, Carline: seeds;
Valerian, Red: late flowers;
Wall Lettuce: seeds;
Woodsage: seedhead.

Total number of plants recorded in the Diaries for September: FP 11, PS 18, CY 13, BO 14, IW 16.

White Bryony & Goosegrass

Betty Mills

October

The real change comes this month and all the beautiful colours of Autumn must be recorded! In the diaries the pages glow with colour:
Sycamore, Ash, Rowan, Beech, Maples - Norway and Japanese, Oak, Chestnut, Service Tree and Elder.
Travellers Joy - Old Man's Beard - cascades over trees, bushes and hedgerows in silver seedhead shrouds.
Bracken changes to gold and then to Rust.
Gorse flowers even more strongly
and Ivy prepares to flower.
There are many late flowerings - Thirteen varieties in the Churchyard alone and more berries ripening and Fungi appearing.
Illustrated, right, some October favourites:
Top: The Queen of October fruits: Sloe berries on Blackthorn; continuing clockwise: an Honesty seedhead; an attempt to draw Old Man's Beard; Acorns and the dramatic fruit of Iris Foetidissima whose sharp, sword-like leaves and curious yellow-mauve flowers are found all over this area.

OTHER PLANTS RECORDED IN THE DIARIES FOR OCTOBER:

TREES:
Alder, Evergreen Oak, Hawthorn, Oak Apples, Sycamore Fruit and Whitebeam berries.

BUSHES:
Flowering Currant leaves & Quinces, Blackberries, Hips, Haws, Laurel & Honeysuckle berries. Burdock Seedheads and Cotoneaster berries.

FUNGI at Pensychnant.

FLOWERS:
Thirteen in the Churchyard:
Buttercup; Crp. Cinquefoil; Clover, Red; Dandelion; Herb Robert; Hogweed; Medick, black; Meadow Vetchling; Ox-eye Daisy; Sowthistle, perennial; Wall Lettuce & Yarrow.

Elsewhere - with some of the above:
Chickweed, Carline Thistle, Burnet Rose, Foxglove, Woodsage, Hedge Mustard (the last three seedheads).

Approx. total of plants recorded in all Diaries for October:
FP7, PS17, CY13, 8015, IW11.

Centre: opening Ivy Flower surrounded by Three HEATHS from late summer:
l to r. Cross-leaved Heath, Bell Heather: ERICA & Ling: CALLUNA

Betty Mills

November

The beginning of the dormant period but Fungi, late berries, turning leaves and evergreens add colour and interest. Illustrated, right, a brief study of Fungi and Evergreens: Examples of the four main types of Fungi recorded in the diaries exclude the False Chanterelle and another large, red-topped inedible one found at Pensychnant. Each group is named on the drawing. (There are 100,000 species worldwide: 10,000 in the UK) The same applies to the Evergreens: The Hemlock and Norway Spruce grow at Pensychnant; the Pines and Cypresses in all locations and the Western Red Cedar and the Yew in the Churchyard.

IN THE DIARIES FOR NOVEMBER:

Flowers on a Path:
Fairyring Champignons, late flowering Sowthistle, turning leaves of Silver Poplar and Turkey Oak and, low in the grass: new leaf growth of Alexanders, Hogweed, Nettle and Goosegrass.

Pensychnant:
Fungi: all varieties of Fungi shown opposite except Puffballs (recorded in August & December) plus the Chantarelles mentioned above. Turning leaves, oak galls and late flowers of: Foxglove, Cambrian Poppy, Herb Robert, Buttercup, Gorse, Bell Heather and Ragwort. PLUS Ivy flowers and five cultivated bushes: Fuschia, Mallow, Hypericum (bud), and Viburnum Fragrans. Also Berberis leaves.

The Churchyard Diary records Black Bryony berries, Ivy flowers, turning leaves of Sycamore, Prunus leaves and flower buds and photographs of the whole churchyard in Autumn including one showing the paths carpeted with fallen Yewberries.

The Eightieth Year Diary in typical, self-indulgent fashion, glories in a late, pale Honeysuckle drawn with a spray of flowering Potato Vine: SOLANUM JASMINOIDES and Ivy flowers and fruit, some ferns, turning Sycamore leaves and a garden bouquet of late flowers: Nasturtium, Daisy, Viburnum and Heather with some Hawkweed and Groundsel thrown in for good measure.

Footpath II: The Invalids Walk shows new leaves of Vetch, Alexanders, Crpg. Cinquefoil, Bindweed and Cotoneaster, some Moss, Fennel Seedheads, Bramble leaves plus two colourful drawings of a Ceanothus and Fuschia Fulgens still flowering in the Haulfre Gardens. There is also a 2-page panoramic drawing of the Orme and the Walk as seen from the Authors' Living-room window.

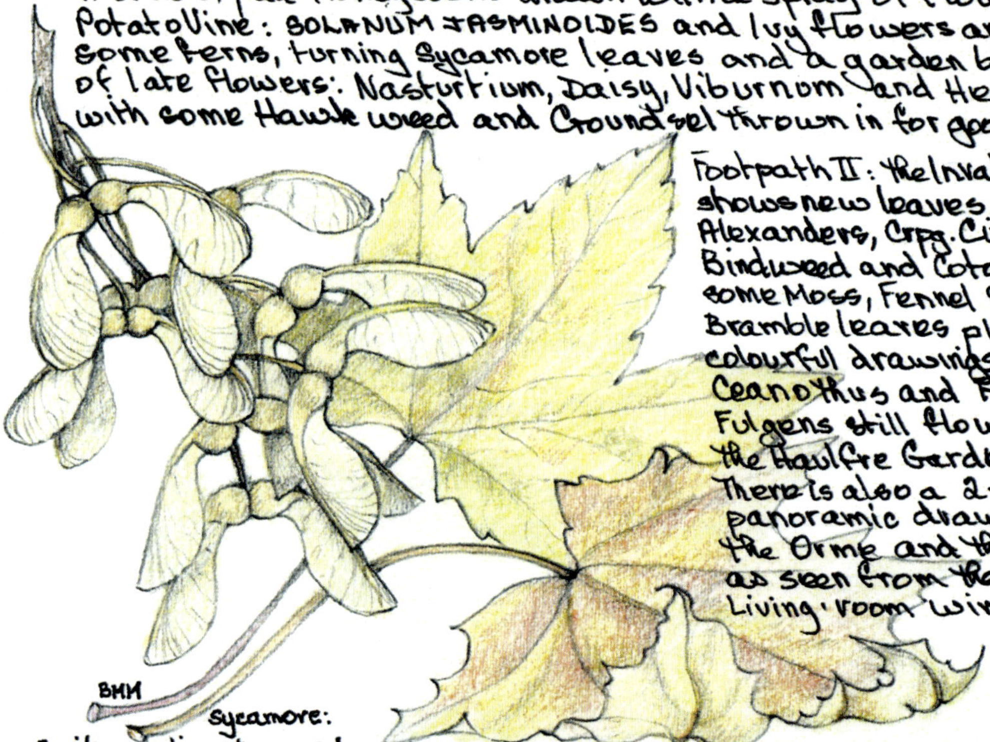

Sycamore:
Fruit & curling & turning leaves.

Champignon
Pinus:
Thuja:
Western Red Cedar
Tsuga: Hemlock
Scots Pine
Puffballs
Honey Fungus
Cypress:
Taxus:
Picea:
Leyland
Monterey
English Yew
Irish Yew
Norway Spruce
Mushrooms
Betty Mills

December

So to the last month of the year and the end of this attempt to share the pleasure of plants – mostly wild and indigenous – and the satisfaction of drawing them.

Four of the Diaries have full-page drawings of Holly and Ivy for this month. The Flowers on a Path just shows the beautifully coloured autumn leaves of Bramble with red-touched Ivy leaves.
Pensychnant Diary has a page of Mosses (see February in this book) and Fungi and adds Pine, Mahonia and Jasmine (see January) to a double-page spread of Holly and Ivy.
In the Churchyard Diary early flowering Prunus (again see January for all these things are still flowering then) some late Daisies and Buttercups are added to the Holly, with Ivy and other evergreens on a second page of photographs.
Eightieth Year includes a panoramic drawing – on red paper – of the Haulfre Gardens trees, a study page of Pine and Cypress and another branch of flowering Prunus with the Holly and Ivy.
Flowers on a Path II adds budded twigs, catkins and dormant gorse buds before a page of Holly and Ivy.

So, illustrated, right: Holly: ILEX AQUIFOLIUM and
Ivy: HEDERA HELIX

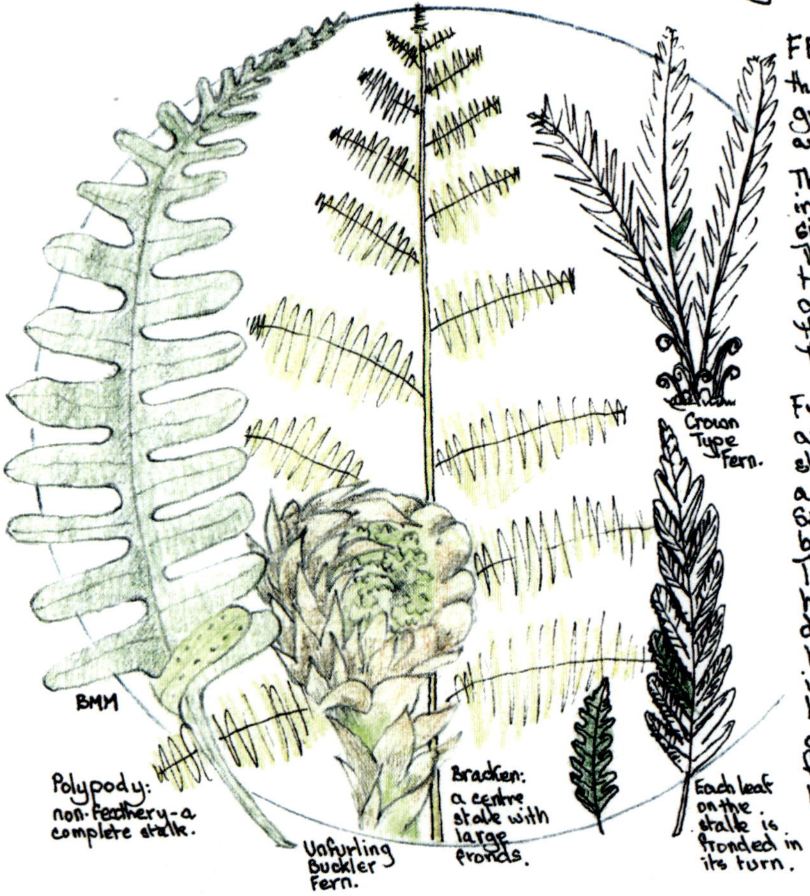

FERNS
the last of the non-flowering group – Fungi (page 28), Moss and Lichen (page 10).

There are 50 species of Fern in the UK from one inch to six feet in height.
The Pensychnant Diary features several species with comparative drawings and there is a page of notes in the Churchyard Diary.

Fern fronds, or leaves, are arranged alternately up the stalk and each frond is like a miniature of the main Fern. Spores on the frond backs can be rust or green.
The drawings, left, show how the Polypody Fern is different from the others; how Bracken grows from individual stalks; how Lord, Lady, King and Buckler, all DRYOPTERIS, grow from the familiar crown; and how beautifully they all unfurl!

Betty Mills

A Note on Plant Families

All plants are classified into Families, the various members of each sharing some characteristics, often the method of propagation or growth habit. Some are listed as in a particular genus or sub-species. In this book the family names are given in the text for most of the plants illustrated and English and Latin names (and Welsh in "The Celebration of Weeds") are included for all.

A good text-book or Plant Dictionary will list all the families, genera and other scientific terminology connected with what can be a very absorbing study.

Here are one or two interesting Plant Family facts:

The largest family is the Daisy family: Compositae; The Carrot family: Umbelliferae includes all the distinctive, umbrella-like flowers of another large family, with the Cabbage family: Cruciferae, claiming many common, four-petalled flowers.

An intriguing fact involves Bryony plants: White Bryony: BRYONIA CRETICA, is in the Cucumber family: CUCURBITACEAE, but Black Bryony: TAMUS COMMUNIS, an equally graceful climbing plant, is the only British member of the Yam family: DIOSCOREACEAE.

Two families with names to conjour with are: HIPPOCASTANCEAE – the Horse Chestnut family, and ZANNICHELLIACEAE – Pond Weed. Plus GRAMINEAE – Grass family! All derived from Greek.

B.M.M.

A Celebration of Weeds

Text and Drawings
by
Betty Mills

A weed is a wild herb growing where it is not wanted.

Oxford Dictionary

If fowering wild herbs growing where they are not wanted are weeds, then trees, shrubs, bushes, grasses, mosses, ferns, fungi and lichen doing the same thing are weeds too.

The rampant, uncontrolled growth of a cascading plant of Ivy-leaved Toadflax rooted in the mortar of a brick wall and intermingled with Hedge Bindweed in full flower was such an inspiring sight one summer's day, that the idea for a project to Celebrate Weeds was born.

Man has discovered over the years what creation has given him in these jewels of nature and some of their valuable qualities are highlighted here:

Culinary, Medicinal, Cultural and simply Artistically Inspirational.

Two plants are included to represent the value of wild plants as animal and insect food: namely Mullein and White Horehound; six of the many plants used for natural dye-stuffs; several for their valuable medicinal qualities which includes, of course, Foxgloves, others, such as Tansy, for food flavouring; and some purely for their inspirational shapes and colours which, surely, includes them all.

Weeds in an urban environment are particularly interesting and it is quite rewarding to look at what is growing between the paving stones and on the bricks and stones of boundary walls on one's daily journeys.

Have you noticed the flourishing Dandelion plant at the bottom of the entry wall in some of the opening shots of Coronation Street?

This chapter demonstrates the fun a Designer can have putting together a project of this kind - choice of colour, shape and presentation - clearly demonstrated here by the twelve geometrical shapes.

The Twelve Shapes

In each of the twelve drawings illustrating this project a geometrical shape has been used to set off the design:
Circle, Triangle, Horizontal Rectangle, Round-cornered Square, Square, Half-circle, Vertical Rectangle, Vertical Oval, Pentagon, Horizontal Oval, Octagon and Diamond

The shapes have no special significance and are just the instinctive choice of the artist.

The subtleties of the Primary, Secondary and Tertiary colours plus three tints - silver grey, mauve and pink - also have no special meaning and have been arranged to enhance the shapes and the plants.
e.g. The Pink Pentagon repeats the shape of the tiny tops on the Ivy Berries and the two shapes of the colour represent the two beautiful dyestuffs produced by the plants.

When this project was exhibited twelve other drawings using the twelve shapes were also shown as a complementary idea.

B.M.M.

The Silver-Grey Circle
Hedge Bindweed and Ivy-leaved Toadflax

These are the two plants which inspired this project. The Hedge Bindweed is a member of the Bindweed or CONVOLVULA Family and has several equally lovely cousins: Sea, Field, Great and Hairy Bindweed, all with the same graceful habit.

The dainty little Ivy-leaved Toadflax named CYMBALARIA MURALIS for its leaf shapes and habit of growing on walls, is a member of the large Figwort or SCROPHULARIA family. The plant has spread all over the British Isles since it escaped from rock gardens after being introduced from the Mediterranean area as long ago as 1640 AD!

A Celebration of Weeds

Common Mallow : MALVA SILVESTRIS &
Lady's Smock : CARDAMINE PRATENSIS
Welsh: Hocysen Gyffredon & Blodyn-y-Gog.
Inspirational leaf & petal shapes &
Medicinal qualities of Mallow.

The Saffron Horizontal Rectangle

Common Mallow and Lady's Smock.

The Mallow family is MALVACEAE and the Lady's Smock - often called Cuckoo Flower - is a Cress (cousins Bittercress and Watercress, among others) in the Cabbage family: CRUCIFERAE.

Both are included here for their beauty but Mallow has Medicinal qualities as well. According to the old Herbals it was used as a relief from Hangovers and for Day Long Calm. More recently to treat wasp stings (the leaves) and make soothing poultices.

However, Lady's Smock leaves do make a safe substitute for watercress.

Above: The Orange Round-Cornered Square
Tansy and Scarlet Pimpernel
Top right: The Soft Sage Half Circle
Germander Speedwell and Welsh Poppy
Bot. right: The Sage Green Square
Rosebay Willowherb and Hedge Mustard

The Special Qualities of these six plants are listed on the Summary on Pages 45 and 46, meanwhile, here are some other claims to fame:

* The Ancient Greeks believed that drinking an infusion of Tansy would lead to immortality.
* The Scarlet Pimpernel was the undercover name of Sir Percy Blakeney in Baroness Orczy's novels of the French Revolution.
* The Latin name for Speedwells: VERONICA, is taken from St. Veronica who wiped the sweat from Christ's face.
* Welsh Poppies are named MECONOPSIS because their seedheads resemble Greek NOT Oriental Poppies.
* Rosebay Willowherb is called Fireweed because of its habit of spreading rapidly where there has been fire as in London during the bombing in the 1939-45 War.
* SISYMBRIUM for Hedge Mustard is just a name - not the usual descriptive Latin!

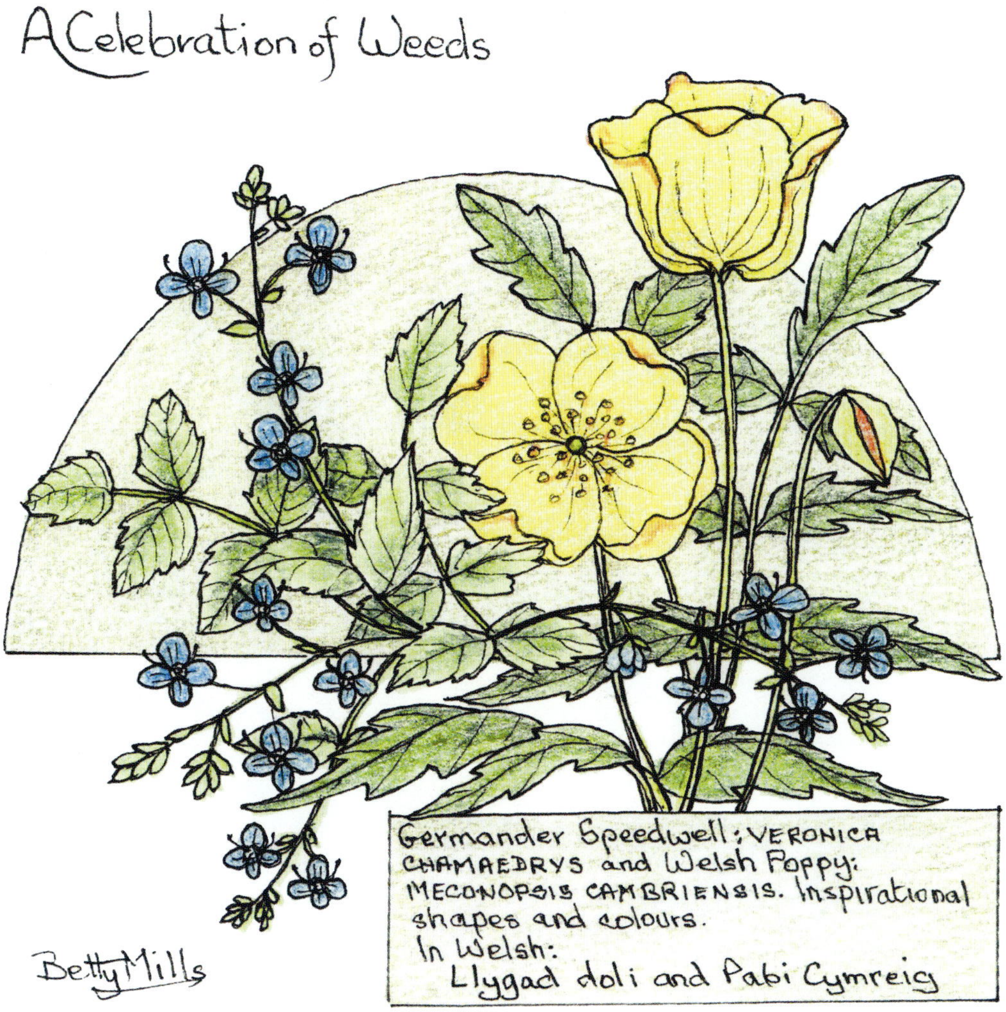
A Celebration of Weeds
Germander Speedwell; VERONICA CHAMAEDRYS and Welsh Poppy: MECONOPSIS CAMBRIENSIS. Inspirational shapes and colours.
In Welsh:
Llygad doli and Pabi Cymreig
Betty Mills

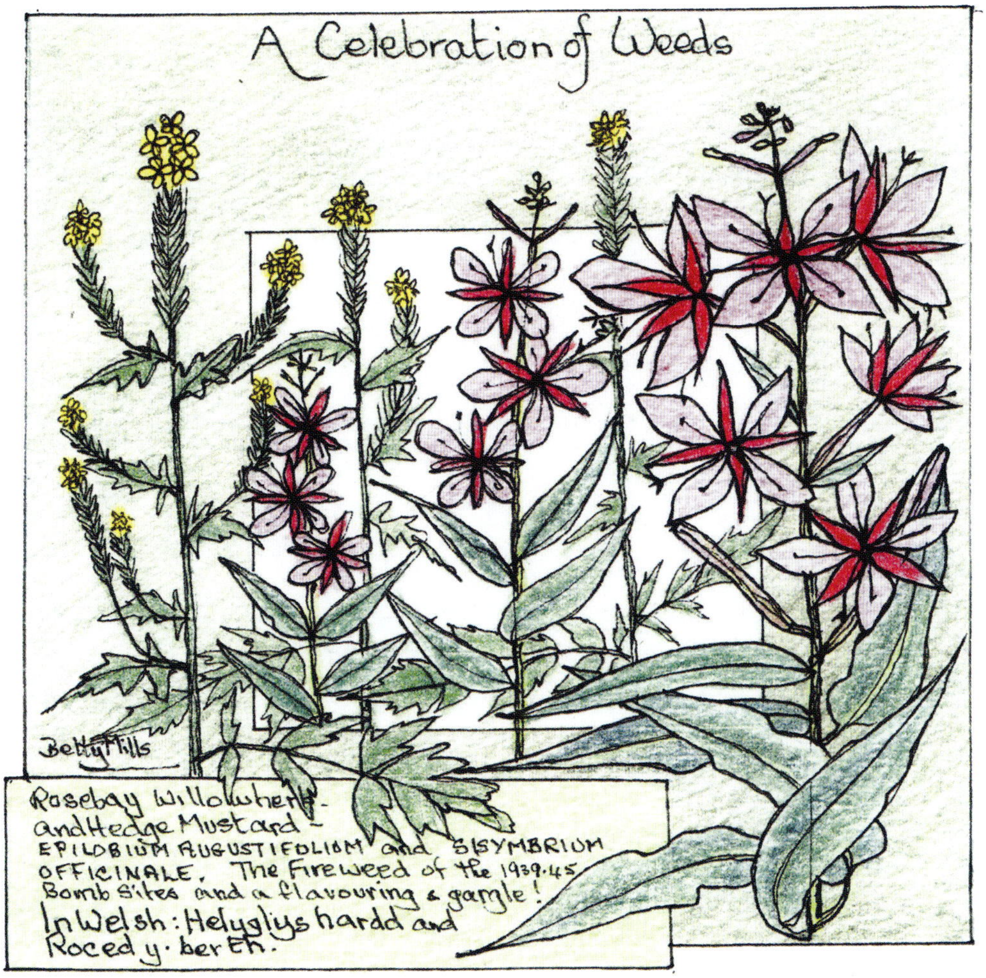
A Celebration of Weeds
Betty Mills
Rosebay Willowherb and Hedge Mustard - EPILOBIUM AUGUSTIFOLIUM and SISYMBRIUM OFFICINALE. The Fireweed of the 1939.45 Bomb Sites and a flavouring & gargle!
In Welsh: Helyglys hardd and Roced y berth.

Above: The Red Triangle: Herb Robert and Eyebright
Two plants with important medicinal qualities - the Eyebright is in use today. Herb Robert is also an example of the Medieval "Doctrine of Signatures": red leaves in Autumn mean it is good for blood disorders. EUPHRASIA, the Latin name for Eyebright means "good cheer" or "to gladden".

Top Right: The Mauve Vertical Oval, Great and Moth Mullein and Red Clover with the Moth & Larva
Both Mullein and Clover have traditional medicinal uses as well as being important Insect Food. Mullein is often called Aaron's Rod or, simply, Verbascum when cultivated. Clover, of course, is beloved of Honey Bees and also used as animal fodder.

Bot. Right: The Purple Vertical Rectangle, Foxglove and White Horehound with the Horehound Plume Moth.
Foxglove: DIGITALIS PURPUREA is currently used for Heart disease. The Horehound was a treatment for coughs and colds.
There are many Folk Tales about both of these - not least that Foxgloves are Fairies' hats and Digitalis does mean "thimble". In Welsh it is Bysedd y cŵn: dog's glove.

A Celebration of Weeds

Mullein Moth.
SHARGACUCULLIA VERBASCUM

a good sized and beautiful creature Easily seen on both yellow varieties of Mullein in the wild and in gardens, with the spotted Larva enjoying the downy leaves.

A Celebration of Weeds

White Horehound Plume Moth:
WHEELERI SPILODACTYLUS

small and unobtrusive. Arrived in North Wales with White Horehound when Cistercian Monks brought the valuable healing herb to the area in 1176 AD.

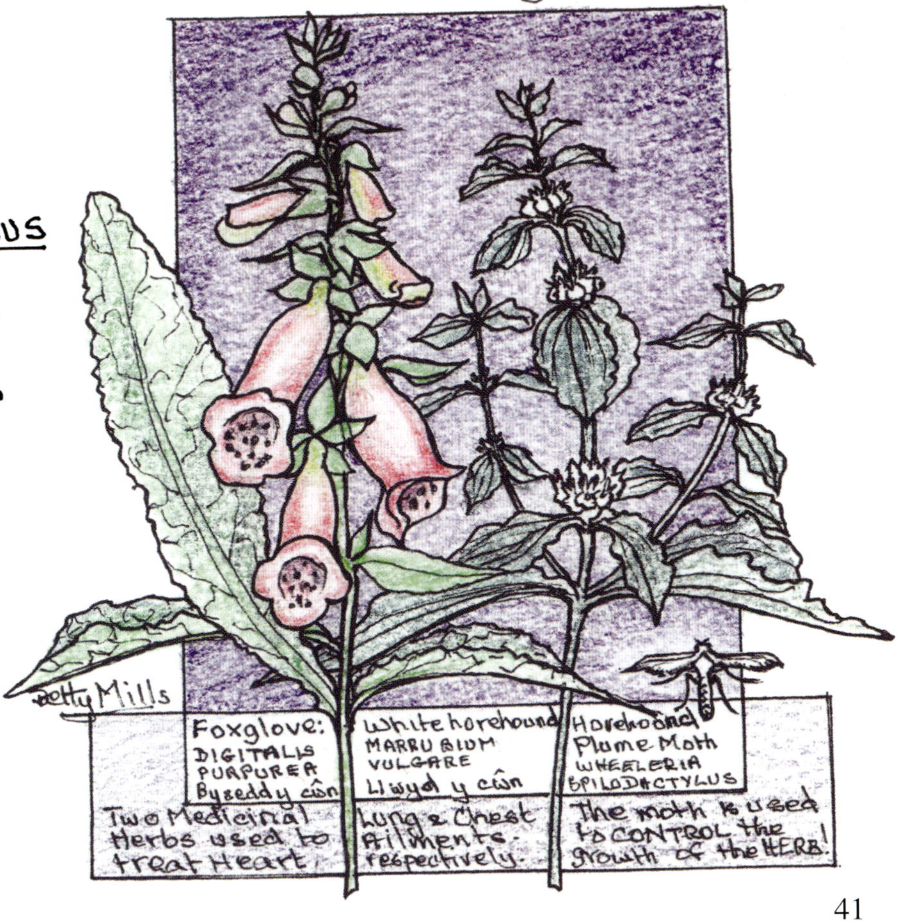

Above: The Blue Octagon - Elder and Blackthorn
Top right: The Yellow Horizontal Oval - Meadowsweet and Broad-leaved Dock
Bottom right: The Pink Pentagon - Ivy Berries and Goosegrass

The special qualities of all six of these plants are listed in the summary on pages 45 and 46 - all of them are a source of dyestuffs which are used today, particularly in hand-weaving: Elder and Blackthorn for Blues, Meadowsweet and Dock for fresh yellow and ochre, respectively. Ivy Berries for soft, dark, mauvish pink and Goosegrass for a strong, vibrant pink.

Other uses:
Elder wood for Penny Whistles,
Blackthorn for Walking Sticks,
Sweet smelling Meadowsweet was used to flavour Mead and calm fevers,
Dock is still used to soothe Nettle stings, scalds & burns.
Ivy flowers in Autumn and Berries in Spring,
and as for Goosegrass - or Cleavers - geese love it and the seeds, when roasted, make a substitute for coffee!

A Celebration of Weeds

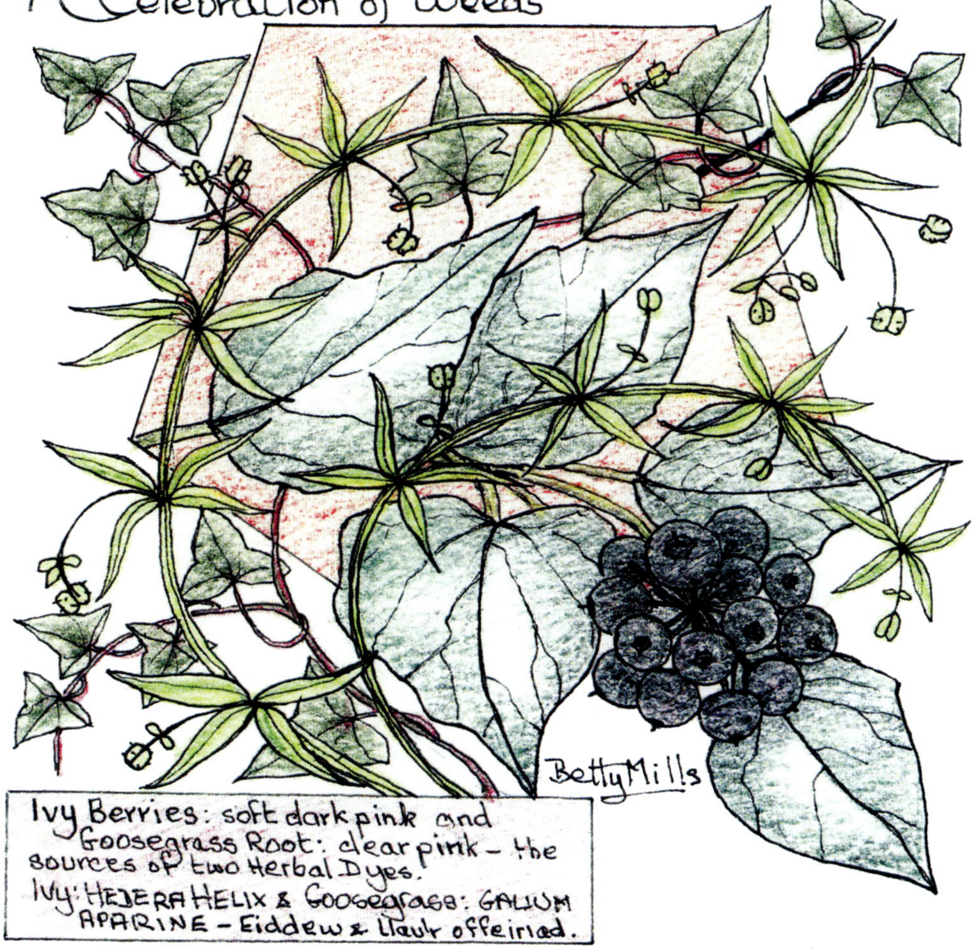

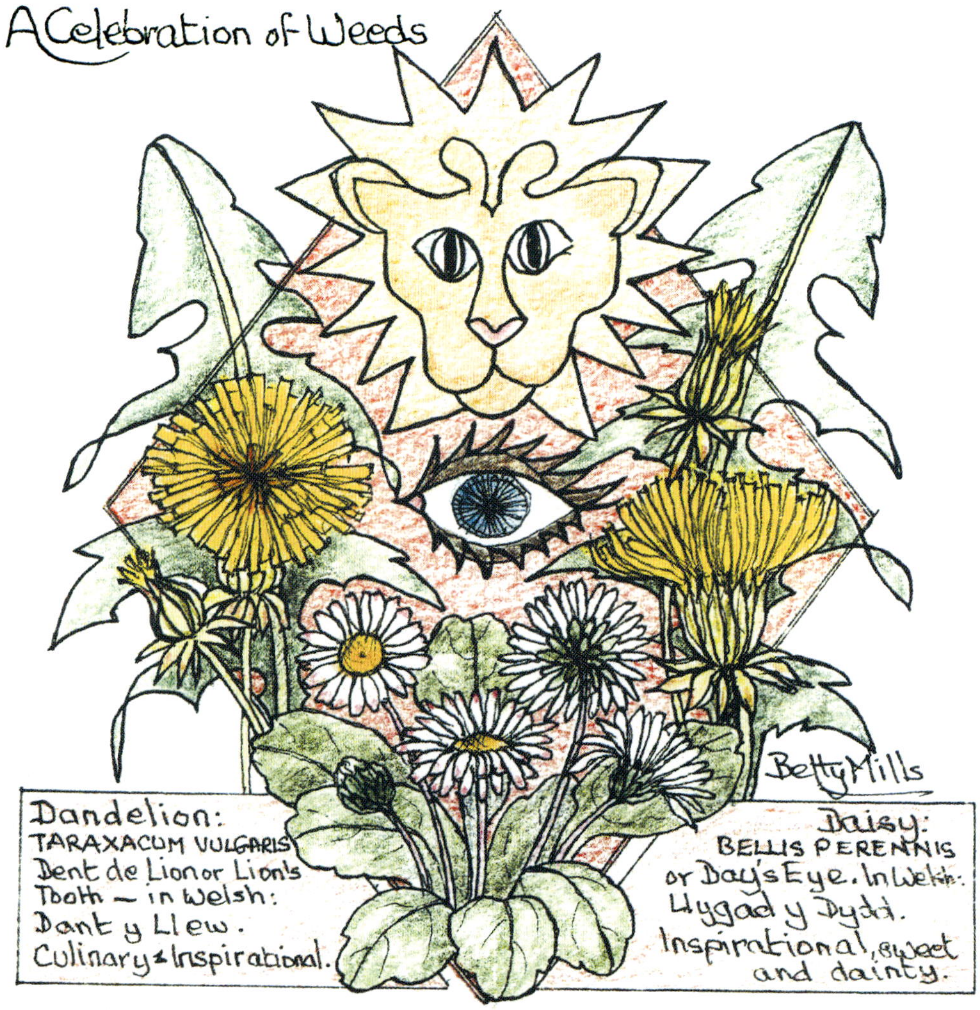

The Bronze Diamond: Dandelion and Daisy

Finally, two of the most common wild plants. Most people can recognise a Dandelion and a Daisy and they are in flower somewhere or another in urban districts throughout the year, popping up on lawns and grass verges and in crevices on paths and pavements. Both have medicinal qualities and the Dandelion has culinary uses.

As for their names:

Dandelion is a version of the French: "Dent du Lion", tooth of the lion, referring to the leaves.

Daisy comes from "day's eye" referring to the daylight opening of the flowers, and its Latin name: BELLIS PERENNIS - "pretty and perennial".

The design above makes the most of these names and forms a cheerful conclusion to this section!

A Summary of some of the SPECIAL QUALITIES displayed by the Wild Plants illustrated herein.

MEDICINAL

most of This information is traditional dating from Medieval Herbals such as Culpepers Herbal published 1653. Two plants marked * are used today.

Dock
for scalds, burns & blisters

Dandelion
for jaundice & consumption

Daisy
for consumption

* Eyebright
for eye ailments - lotion

* Foxglove - Digitalis
for Heart Disease

Goosegrass
for Slimming

Herb Robert
for staunching blood flow

Hedge Mustard
for gargle for vocal ills

Mallow
for hang-overs, poultices
day-long calm & wasp stings

Mullein
for coughs & colds

Meadowsweet
for pain & fevers

Scarlet Pimpernel
for madness & melancholy

Speedwell
for wounds & respiratory complaints

White Horehound
for coughs, chest ailments & as a poison antidote.

Red Clover
for whooping cough

Nicholas Culpeper, physician, 1616-1654.

CULINARY

Current uses:

Blackthorn Berries
for SLOE GIN

Dandelion flowers
for DANDELION WINE
- leaves
for Salads: Vitamin A & C

Elder flowers
for ELDER CHAMPAGNE

Elder berries
for ELDERBERRY WINE

Goosegrass seeds
for COFFEE (when roasted)

Lady's Smock leaves
for WATERCRESS substitute

Tansy leaves
for FLAVOURING

INSECT & WILDLIFE FOOD

particularly -

Ivy: flowers - nectar in the autumn - bees
berries - in spring - birds & the Holly Blue butterfly caterpillars.

Mullein - Great & Moth:
food for the Mullein Moth

Red Clover: bees and for animal fodder

Rosebay Willowherb:
seeds for insects

White Horehound:
food for the Horehound Plume Moth

INSPIRATIONAL

all the plants in this study are inspirationally beautiful to the artist & designer, but especially -

DAISY
for charm, freshness & simplicity

DANDELION
for leaf shapes, flower structure & seedheads

ELDER
for flowers, leaves, fruit & autumn colour

BLACKTHORN
for flowers on leafless branches and blue.black sloe berries

HEDGE & all BINDWEEDS
for fascinating growth, flower & leaf shapes

IVY. LEAVED TOADFLAX
for leaf & flower shapes & charm of habit

MEADOWSWEET
for the whole plant

ROSEBAY WILLOWHERB
for shape of whole plant & for seedheads

SPEEDWELLS - all
for colour of flowers & leaf shapes

WELSH POPPY
for the whole plant

CULTURAL

As the Source of DYES most wild plants can be used - in this study the following six are highlighted:

BROAD.LEAVED DOCK
Leaves: dark yellow

BLACKTHORN BERRIES
- blue

ELDERBERRIES - blue

MEADOWSWEET
- fresh yellow

GOOSEGRASS root - strong pink

IVY BERRIES - Mauvish pink

FOLKLORE

many stories are recorded some in the text herein. Plants concerned:

IVY - power to dispel house goblins

TANSY - the greeks believed it could bring eternal life

ROSEBAY WILLOWHERB - nicknamed Fireweed

WHITE HOREHOUND
story re Cistercian monks

HERB ROBERT
DAISY
DANDELION
SPEEDWELL

How did they get their names?

An ALPHABET of Flowers

The record of a Design Project

Text and Drawings
by

Betty Mills

Introduction

Human beings communicate by means of words - whatever their language, race, colour, age, state of mind and body.
Words are made up of letters.
Letters are arranged in Alphabets.

ALPHABET: set of letters used in a language or symbols or signs for them. (Oxford Dictionary).

First two letters, or "characters", of the Greek Alphabet are:
ALPHA BETA.

Pictures are used to communicate too: wall paintings in caves were added to the grunts and gestures of early man.
By the time the Ancient Egyptians were established, with a very sophisticated way of life, words and pictures were combined in hieroglyphics. The Oxford Dictionary definition is both revealing and fascinating:

HIEROGLYPHIC: Figure of an object standing for a word, syllable or sound, as used in Ancient Egyptian and other writing.

Modern languages of the Western World have all evolved gradually over time mainly from the two Classical languages of the Ancient World: Latin and Greek. Many languages use the classical Latin 26-letter A to Z alphabet and the shapes of the letters are based on Roman forms.
The Greek ALPHA to OMEGA list of 24 characters has, mostly, differently shaped letters also reflected in such alphabets as Russian and Arabic.
The shapes and forms of Japanese and Chinese writing and the symbols used by many more primitive or more recently-evolved peoples, are special studies in themselves.

So, in modern, bi-lingual Wales we use English with the Roman alphabet and Welsh with the Early mid-European Celtic alphabet. Both Roman and Celtic typefaces are used in both languages.
The Celtic letters owe much to the beautiful Medieval manuscripts such as the Book of Kells in Dublin and the Lindisfarne Gospels. Olde Englishe letters from other early manuscripts are another very decorative source.

Once one gets into a subject study and realises the vital importance of correct terminology and precise meanings and descriptions then language and letters begin to take on a new interest. Drawing Wild Flowers and wanting to be absolutely clear about which one you are portraying is a case in point.

Deciding - for the third time - to make an Alphabet of Wild Flowers - this time as twenty-six individual pictures each featuring a single letter - brought a number of interests together especially from the Design point of view.
Deciding to make A4 drawings, using a variety of paper, pen, pencil, water-colour, pencil crayon and other media, making the letter a large part of the design sometimes with background shapes, came naturally.

But what typeface for the letter?
What language for the plant name? Latin or English? Or should Welsh be used?
What about Plant Families?
And so the fascination of research began.

The result was a decision to use a Latin name for one flower in each design and an English name for the other (sometimes there is more than one of each, but they are alternated so that the first one for A is English and the first one for B is Latin and so on until the first one for Z is Latin). However, they are all properly cross-referenced as it is the Latin names for wild plants that are universally recognised and should be clear and without doubt.
Many English names are based on folk nick-names for the plants and vary from district to district - even from botanist to botanist, but the Latin names are sacrosanct!
All This has led to unexpected combinations of flowers and plants in one picture which has sometimes been contrary to my usual practice of only drawing flowers together which would be IN flower together.

So: Design number one for A is a strongly-shaped Celtic letter with Alexanders (SMYRNIUM OLUSATRUM) for English and ARMERIA MARITIMA (Sea Thrift) for Latin with Sea Arrowgrass (plant family JUNCAGINACEAE, to complete a Plant Family A-Z.

This project was a pleasure to carry out and it is hoped that it will add to the readers' interest in wild plants, conservation, words, languages, letters, design and - not least of all - colour.

Betty Mills

A Alexanders: SMYRNIUM OLUSATRUM (Carrot family), ARMERIA MARITIMA: Sea Thrift (Sea Lavender family) and Sea Arrowgrass: TRIGLOCHIN MARITIMA (Arrowgrass family) to complete a Latin Alphabet of Plant Families). Pen and water-colour design with a Celtic capital.

B for Latin: BELLIS PERENNIS: Daisy (Daisy or COMPOSITAE family) and four for English: Bluebell: ENDYMION NON-SCRIPTUS; Birdsfoot Trefoil: LOTUS CORNICULATUS; left, White Bryony: BRYONIA CRETICA, Cucumber family and, right, Black Bryony: TAMUS COMMUNIS, the only British member of the Yam family (DIOSCOREACEAE). Pencil and pencil crayon with a Roman capital.

2 BELLIS PERENNIS: Daisy - COMPOSITAE: Daisy Family with Bluebells: ENDYMION NON SCRIPTUS, Bird's foot Trefoil: LOTUS CORNICULATUS and two Bryonys - left: white: BRYONIA CRETICA (Cucumber Family) and Black: TAMUS COMMUNIS - Yam family

C Cranesbill, Bloody: GERANIUM SANGUINEUM (Geranium family); Creeping Cinquefoil: POTENTILLA REPTANS (Rose family) and CALYSTEGIA SYLVATICA: Hedge Bindweed. (Bindweed or CONVOLVULACEAE family).
Pen, pencil crayon and Conté crayon on Ingres paper with an Old English capital.

D DIGITALIS PURPUREA: Foxglove, Figwort family and Dandelion (Dent du Lion - tooth of Lion): TARAXACUM VULGARE (Daisy Family).
A "manuscript" design in Pen and watercolour with an Old English capital.

E Evening Primrose: OENOTHERA BIENNIS (Willowherb family) and, for Latin, ECHIUM VULGARE: Viper's Bugloss (Borage family).
Pencil and pencil-crayon with a free-hand capital.

5 Evening Primrose: OENOTHERA BIENNIS (common) Willowherb Family and ECHIUM VULGARE: Viper's Bugloss - BORAGINA Family

F A Rose family member for Latin: FILLIPENDULA ULMARIA, the well-named Meadowsweet, with Fennel: FOENICULUM VULGARE (Carrot family). A design of four free-hand capitals using pen, pencil crayon and Conté crayon on Ingrès paper.

G Gorse: ULEX EUROPAEUS (Pea family or LEGUMINOSAE) and the delicate GALIUM VERUM: Lady's Bedstraw (Bedstraw family).
Pen and watercolour with a flowing free-hand capital.

H Five from the same habitat: HELIANTHEMUM NUMMULARIUM, Common Rockrose and Harebell: CAMPANULA ROTUNDIFOLIA with Three Heaths: Ling: CALLUNA VULGARIS, X-leaved Heath: ERICA TETRALIX and Bell Heather: ERICA CINEREA. Pencil and pencil crayon with a Roman capital.

I Ivy: HEDERA HELIX (Ivy family) with IRIS FOETID-ISSIMA: Stinking Iris – winter fruit – (Iris family). Pen and pencil crayon on Ingrés paper with a decorated Roman Capital.

J JUNIPERUS COMMUNIS: Juniper, in the Cyprus family; Jack·go·to·bed·at·noon (which it does!) - Goatsbeard: TRAGOPOGON PRATENSIS, Daisy family and Jack·by·the·Hedge - Garlic Mustard: ALLIARIA PETIOLATA, Cabbage family. Pen and water·colour with a free·hand capital.

K Two High Summer flowers: Knapweed (Black) CENTAUREA NIGRA (Daisy family) and, for Latin, KNAUTIA ARVENSIS: Field Scabious (Teasel family).
Pen and watercolour with a Celtic capital.

L LINARIA VULGARIS: Common Toadflax (Figwort family); LAMIUM ALBUM: White Deadnettle (Deadnettle family); LACTUCA PERENNIS: Blue Lettuce (Daisy family); and for English: Lime: TILIA CORDATA, leaves, flowers & fruit. Pen and pencil crayon with Conté crayon on Ingrès paper with a Roman capital.

12 LINARIA VULGARIS: Common Toadflax, LAMIUM ALBUM: White DeadNettle, LACTUCA PERENNIS: Blue Lettuce and Lime: TILIA CORDATA- families Figwort, Deadnettle, Daisy & Lime respectively

M Milkwort: POLYGALA VULGARIS (Milkwort family), MALVA SYLVESTRIS: Common Mallow (Mallow family), MYOSOTIS ARVENSIS: Field Forget-me-Not (Borage family).
Pen and watercolour with a Celtic-inspired capital as are most of the Free-hand capitals in this study.

13 MALVA SYLVESTRIS: Common Mallow; MYOSOTIS ARVENSIS: Field Forgetmenot and Milkwort, common: POLYGALA VULGARIS

N NARCISSUS PSEUDO NARCISSUS: Wild Daffodil (Daffodil Family: AMARYLLIDACEAE) with Nettle, Stinging: URTICA DIOICA (Nettle family). Pencil and pencil crayon with Roman capitals.

O Ox-eye Daisy: CHRYSANTHEMUM LEUCANTHEMUM (Daisy family) and ORCHIS MASCULATA: Early Purple Orchid (Orchid family).
Pen, pencil crayon and Conte pencil on Ingres paper.

P PICRIS ECHOIDES: Bristly Ox-tongue (Daisy family), PLANTAGO LANCEOLATA: Ribwort Plantain, a bold member of the Plantain family and, for English. Pansy, Wild (Heartsease): VIOLA TRICOLOR. (Violet family) Pen and watercolour with Roman capitals.

Q Quince, Japanese: CYDONIA OBLONGA (Rose family), Quaking Grass: BRIZA MEDIA (Grass family) and, for Latin, QUERCUS PETRAEA: Sessile or Durmast Oak (Beech family).
Pen and watercolour with a Roman capital.

R ROSA CANINA: Dog Rose in the Rose family with RANUNCULUS FICARIA: Lesser Celandine from the Buttercup family with a Lily family member: Ramsoms: ALLIUM URSINUM.
Pen, pencil crayon and Conté pencil on Ingres paper.

S Sea Holly: ERYNGIUM MARITIMUM, Carrot family; Scabious, Devil's Bit: SUCCISA PRATENSIS, Teasel family; and two Pink family members: Stitchwort, Greater: STELLARIA HOLOSTEA and SILENE DIOICA: Red Campion. Pen and watercolour with a free-hand capital.

19 Sea Holly: ERYNGIUM MARITINUM; Stitchwort, Greater: STELLARIA HOLOSTEA; Scabious, Devil's Bit: SUCCISA PRATENSIS and SILENE DIOICA: Red Campion.

T TRIFOLIUM REPENS: White Clover (Pea family); Traveller's Joy (Old Man's Beard): CLEMATIS VITALBA; with two Thistles: Carline: CARLINA VULGARIS and Slender: CARDUUS TENUIFLORUS, both in the Daisy family. Pen + pencil crayon with a Celtic capital.

20
Traveller's Joy: CLEMATIS VITALBA with two Thistles - left Carline: CARLINA VULGARIS & Slender: CARDUUS TENUIFLORUS plus TRIFOLIUM REPTENS: White Clover

U Upright Brome: BROMUS ERECTUS, a Grass family member with UMBILICUS RUPESTRIS: Navel wort in the Stonecrop family (CRASSULACEAE).
Pen and pencil crayon on Ingres paper with an Old English capital.

21 UMBILICUS RUPESTRIS: Navelwort & Upright Brome: BROMUS ERECTUS

V 3 varieties of VERONICA: Speedwell -
V· HEDERIFOLIA: Lilac Ivy·leaved; V· SPICATA: Spiked
and V· PERSICA: Common Field with two Vetches -
Common: VICIA SATIVA and Bush: VICIA SEPIUM,
plus Meadow Vetchling: LATHYRUS PRATENSIS.
Pencil and pencil crayon with a Roman capital.

W A letter in the Medieval, illuminated style: Willowherb (Rosebay): EPILOBIUM AUGUSTIFOLIUM (W'herb family) with WAHLENBERGIA HEDERACEA: Ivy-leaved Bellflower (B'flower family).
Pen and water colour with an Old English capital.

24 XANTHIUM SPINOSUM: Spiny Cocklebur

X The only letter without an English representative – XANTHIUM SPINOSUM: Spiny Cocklebur (Daisy family).
Pen and pencil crayon and Charcoal with a Celtic capital.

Y And this one without a Latin representative - Yew: TAXUS BACCATA (Yew or TAXACEAE family) with Yellow Horned Poppy: GLACIUM FLAVUM (poppy family). Pen and pencil crayon with an old English capital.

Z ZANNICHELLIA PALUSTRIS: Horned Pondweed and Zig-Zag Clover: TRIFOLIUM MEDIUM. The Pondweed in its own family and the clover in the Pea family.
For this final design a flight of fancy using pen and watercolour and a reflected Roman capital.

INDEX

A list of the English names and the universally acknowledged Latin names of all the plants illustrated in This book.

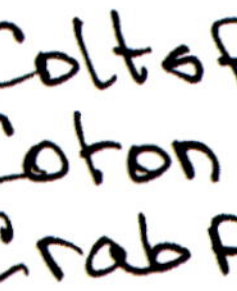

Page

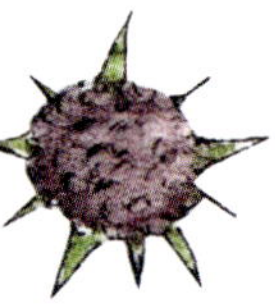